DAVID PORTER

Cycling in Greater Geneva Travel Guide

Explore Greater Geneva by bike and make your experience fun!

First edition

This book was professionally typeset on Reedsy.
Find out more at reedsy.com

Contents

1

Introduction

Welcome to the Greater Geneva Cycle Guide! My name is David Porter and I'm extremely excited to be writing this book! When new friends or family want to go for a cycle I'm going to give them this pocket-sized guide without them having to flip through hundreds of pages of information. I may even print out 20 copies and leave them at the entrance to our home for our visitors!

Another reason I'm happy to write this book is that when I jump on a bike, I feel the freedom of the fresh air in this beautiful part of the world surrounded by fields, forests, mountains and lakes. I'm excited when others get to plan a trip and take advantage of the wonderful area I live in.

You might have moved to Geneva or you're just visiting and want to take a few hours to cycle outside of the city and if you're like me you don't want to do the same trip every time! You might also be thinking apart from around the lake are there any flat cycle paths? Or you're ready to cycle a bit uphill but not too much!

I've been living in the Greater Geneva area (on the French side behind the airport) known as the Pays de Gex for more than 13 years and have commuted by bike both to Geneva and to nearby Founex, Vaud (20km outside the city). I have also cycled right around the lake with my son (and 3000 others) in a day (180km), taken my bike on the boat across to Yvoire and even cycled over the Furka pass in Valais as part of a week-long tour of Switzerland in 2012. On another occasion, I cycled to a meeting in Lausanne on a Saturday morning, took the boat to Thonon to see my dentist and cycled back on the French side of the lake.

Most of my cycling experience, however, is in the greater Geneva area when I have a free hour or two and also when I am not feeling overly fit! Or if I'm keen for a less enthusiastic family member to join me, the question arises: where can we go today?

If you do not have your own bike with you, you may be looking to hire one, or even buy a second-hand bike. You might have questions about traffic, cycling in France, where to eat, what to expect weather-wise depending on the time of year or why Swiss bikes have number plates! My hope is that this simple guide will answer the important questions and steer you in the right direction!

This book will not include every detail or cycle path available but will hopefully give you some clear ideas of possible excursions and what to expect.

If you're looking for a 10-day cycle tour not coming back to the same place at night, then this book isn't for you. I do, however, have links to those who organize such tours if you're thinking about it!

2

The Weather Cycle

The climate of the greater Geneva area has warm summers and cold winters and could be described as 'moderately continental'. While Geneva boasts of having more hours of sunshine than Zurich or Bern (1930 hours annually) the city lies 375m above sea level with average temperatures ranging from maximum temperatures of 27oC (80oF) in July (Minimum of 15oC/57oF) down to a maximum of 5oC(41oF) in January with a minimum of -1oC (30oF). Of course, what it actually feels like on a bike is what we're particularly interested in! I've cycled in 37oC(98oF) in the summer and also in -5oC (23oF) in winter with a strong windchill!

The Geneva lake (known locally as 'Lac Léman') seems to invite its own weather system at times and one can often see clouds hover around the mountains on either the Alps or the Jura side. The rain can be very wet! Precipitation is recorded at 925 millimetres (36.5 inches) per year. The Atlantic depressions are rarer in the summer, but you need to be prepared for possible thunderstorms which can break out in the afternoons! As with any cycling trip, it's always best to check the weather forecast and be prepared! You'll want to check what the

4

'bise' is doing, the northeast wind which makes the lake choppy and will have an impact on your lakeside excursions. It can be quite rainy from September to November although still very pleasant for a ride.

On the whole, it's never too hot to cycle, and even in the middle of a hot summer, these shorter trips are totally doable in the morning or evening!

I don't know how many cities have people cycling in the snow, but with around 30cm (12.5 inches) per year in Geneva, several hardened commuters can be seen cycling in the snow, while most people take the tram or the bus.

While mid-May to mid-September may be the best time for excursions for those of us who live here, we can have great and very pleasant cycles in February as well as November.

3

Natural environment - The lie of the land

I 'm not a scientist but I do appreciate the varied and beautiful nature of the valley between the Jura and the Alps.

The Pays de Gex, the area behind the airport which stretches from Divonne to Bellegarde along the base of the Jura mountains, is a rich habitat for birdlife and forest animals. It is not uncommon to see several birds of prey encircling a particular field or small forest and even private gardens.

As a road cyclist, I'm not often cycling in actual forests although friends who do more mountain biking have a whole range of options to avail from as the area is so rich in various types of forest. For those who do not mind the climb, the Col de la Faucille (1323m) above the town of Gex (600m) offers a beautiful mountain pass with stunning views of Mont Blanc across the lake. There are a lot of options for deep forest and mountain trails for either hiking or mountain biking. The local ski station of Monts Jura has two main cable car ascents either directly from Crozet behind St Genis Pouilly or from the top of La Faucille where mountain biking is available in the summer months.

The area west of the Geneva state (Geneva is one of 27 Swiss states) sitting in the middle between the Salève and the Jura (both of which are in France), is largely made up of vineyards and quaint little villages. While some of it is flat, there are small hills meandering the relief, leading through picturesque villages crossing the Rhone river back and forth.

The Salève on the South West side of the city also offers cycling opportunities with vast fields along the summit with areas of forest above what appears to be a hard rock face near the cable car which, like Monts-Jura, is also cyclist-friendly.

The rich forest vegetation along the south side of Lake Geneva basin (Evian direction) offers a peaceful break to the cyclist at one of the small ports or beaches before arriving at the beautiful medieval village of Yvoire.

4

Pre-Trip Planning

Where to stay

This cycling guide is not a general travel guide but should you be looking for accommodation outside of the usual hotels or hostels, many good Airbnbs outside of the city in smaller villages should be able to offer space to park your bike protected from the elements.

There are cheaper accommodation options in the Pays de Gex on the French side such as Ferney-Voltaire or the St Genis Pouilly area or in Annemasse on the south side of Geneva either in hotels, Airbnbs or the more traditional 'chambres d'hôtes'. Cycling tour specialists will offer their own accommodation as part of their package.

Bike Hire

If you do not have your own bike with you, there are a whole host of rental options in Geneva and in neighbouring towns on either side of the French border. I will mention three options.

For the serious cyclist, *Bike Switzerland*, which offers Jura and Alpine tours throughout the country has a wide range of specialised bikes available at their rental shop in Geneva. At the time of writing, a hybrid, gravel, or E-bike will cost 70CHF for a day or 170CHF for 4 days.

(see https://bikeswitzerland.com/ for further information).

Another option is *Geneva Cycling* where a road or E-bike bike can be hired for 40EUR for a day, or around 100EUR for 3 days. A hybrid can be rented at only 25EUR daily, or 55Euros for 3 days. They are located in Gaillard, just across the border on the south side. According to their website, they can deliver to you where you are (for an additional cost). Like others, they can assist you with group day trips.

(see https://genevacycling.com/road-bike-rental/ for further information).

A local and popular option is through *Geneva roule*, a non-profit organisation, (open 7 days a week) where, at the time of writing, a touring or electric bike will cost 28CHF or 38CHF per day. (a city bike hire costs 14CHF/day) There are three different sites and often what is not available from one is available from another.

(see https://www.geneveroule.ch/en/rent-and-loan/for further information).

Bike Purchase

There are many specialized cycle shops in the area. If you're looking to buy a second-hand bike, Charly's, rue de Lausanne in Geneva has some excellent reviews. A google list of cycle shops for either well priced new bikes or second hand can be easily found. It is not uncommon to find villages advertise a 'bourse aux velos', a bring and buy sale of second-hand bikes. These tend to be cheaper on the French side of the border. There are also several Facebook groups which sell bikes from time to time including *Geneva Expats* or *For sale free or wanted in Vaud/Geneva*. You can also check out the cycle shops I include below.

Road safety

Most of the lake areas have separate cycle paths, although care is needed especially in urban areas at crossings even when cyclists have their separate traffic lights. Cars turning right (and therefore parallel to you) are required to give way if you are on a cycle path and you wish to go straight on. All of this needs to be 'negotiated' and must be taken with great care. A mark on my upper lip, a workday lost and bike repairs are testimony of a car not giving way nor indicating to change direction at the last moment!

Most of the cycle paths, especially out of town, are separate from traffic but it is important to look out for pedestrians who, despite the clear markings, are not always aware that they share the footpaths. Most of the cycle trips mentioned in this book are either on cycle paths or on very quiet roads where especially in France, cars will usually give you a wide berth.

Neither Switzerland nor France has made helmets compulsory but their use is highly recommended. In Switzerland, drinking and cycling are treated the same as drinking and driving a car with a limit of 50mg/100ml of alcohol. Should you cause an accident for any reason in Switzerland you will receive a fine for not being in control of your bike!

Question: Is a bell necessary on a bike? Swiss answer: Only if it's electric. It is recommended however to have one in Geneva and you will hear them used on cycle paths by other cyclists.

Emergencies

In the unlikely event of an accident, the European phone number for both France and Switzerland is 112. Medical costs of European and Swiss citizens are covered providing you are from elsewhere in Europe and have an EHIC (European Health Insurance Card) although you may have to pay for an ambulance and claim the cost back through insurance.

If you live in Switzerland and own a bike you need to register it and also buy an annual vignette, (yes like the motorway one but cheaper), which includes compulsory third-party insurance. Short-term visitors don't need to worry about this. If you live in France, check with your home insurance if you are normally covered for bike accidents through the personal liability mechanism.

Theft

Unfortunately, bike theft is a massive problem in the city of Geneva itself. Always make sure you have a very good lock and take advantage of dedicated bike park areas. While this is less of an issue outside the city, it is naturally a good idea to always lock your bike well.

5

What to bring

Depending on the length of your trip it's always useful to wear adapted clothing for cycling. If you do not have cycling gear, wear a bright T-shirt (for visibility) or fleece (depending on the time of year) and shorts or light trousers (you will get warm). It is always better to wear gloves (even in summer) for protection, warmth and visibility. If your bike does not have panniers or a rack it is useful to wear a small rucksack for your water bottle, waterproofs and potentially a cycle light (if there is not one fitted), a map if you have one and your phone. The rucksack is also useful to slide your cycle helmet in if you go exploring or visit a restaurant. A pump, spare tubes and a puncture kit with the necessary tools are also important to carry in your bag as there are few bike shops outside of the main towns! Between late November and March, you will probably want to wear some sort of a thin woolly hat under your helmet.

Especially in winter, mudguards on your bike will keep you from getting dirty or overly wet!

6

On the road

You may be looking for a supermarket to purchase some necessities for a day trip because you did not get time to make lunch.

Within Switzerland, the Co-op or Migros are good options. In the Pays de Gex, the three main towns have a variety of Carrefour Market, Intermarché, Leclerc and Val Thoiry also has a Migros. The Annemasse area has the above-mentioned shops and similar to the Pays de Gex also has Lidl and Vival.

If you are visiting, you may wonder about currency questions. In Geneva, it is the Swiss Franc (CHF) while in neighbouring France it is the Euro (EUR). Some supermarkets close to the border in France will accept both Swiss Francs and Euros and various ATMs offer both.

Families

You will see entire families on bikes, sometimes almost all on one bike! With various child seat options in front, including what looks like an attached 'wheelbarrow', child seats behind or in an adjoining trailer allow the transport of quite a few children at the one time! All of this is legal.

For the following suggested routes, families with children who are also cycling, I recommend Route number 1a and 2a, 2b and 6a below.

Cycle Shops in an emergency

While there are several bike shops both in Geneva and in the suburbs, others which have good reviews, some of which I use personally include *Velo Culture, Decathlon, Go Sport* in Val Thoiry. There are mountain bike options at the Crozet télécabine, La Faucille and *MonVTT* in St Cergue. On the other side of Geneva, *Ovelo* for electric bikes, *Veloland* or *Annemasse velos* have good reviews.

Cyclomundo (the same as Genevacycling above) is in Gaillard probably the closest cycle shop to the Saleve Télécabine. *Velometier* in Thonon is not far away from Yvoire.

7

Top 9 Trips (23 possibilities in all)

For 7 of the following 9 rides, I outline 3 possible lengths of excursion, depending on time, energy and difficulty. Some of the longer rides include more hills. Not all the rides are of the same length.

If you wish to cycle only one way, it is possible to take a bike on Swiss public transport (train, boat and some post buses) (a day pass for a bike is 14CHF at the time of writing and cheaper if calculated on a point to point basis for short trips).

I have used links to Google Maps to let you download the route which can be accessed either by clicking on the link under the Route title (if you are reading an E-book) or by scanning the appropriate QR code at the back of the book. (All QR codes are working at the time of publishing.)

Each ride includes various points of interest along the way so that even if you do not want to do the whole ride, you can do part of it and have felt it was fun and definitely worthwhile!

I will begin with the starting point for routes from the Pont du Mont Blanc in Geneva (the main traffic bridge over the Rhone down from the train station) but I will suggest various other well-known starting points, including the CERN Tram terminus (no 18), the car park at the port in Versoix, and the Intermarché in St Genis Pouilly. You can add or subtract whatever time difference you are from these points or your closest point to join a particular route.

Routes 7 and 8 are geared to the more experienced cyclist who does not mind climbing for 9 km at a stretch but will enjoy the reward of the subsequent downhill!

8

North Lake Swiss route

Nyon Castle

- 1a. Geneva-Nyon (22.5km)

- 1b. Geneva-Rolle (34km)
- 1c. Geneva-Morges (49.2km)

1a. Geneva - Nyon port (23 km - one way)

C lick on the link or copy the relevant QR code (chapter 17) to discover the route
https://goo.gl/maps/4L2cMaLSaDdQ9Wve6

Starting Point: Pont du Mont-Blanc, Geneva. This route is, for the most part, on flat cycle paths parallel to the main road and uses part of the Swiss National Cycle Route number 1.

Follow the lake past the Wilson hotel and turn right for Lausanne at the main traffic lights and then keep straight on staying on the cycle paths the whole trip. Check out the following places to visit:

Interesting rest points:

- Versoix-Quai de Versoix (8.9km) - you may have seen pictures of cars frozen over in this street from the winter of 2005 or 2012!
- Versoix-Port-Choiseul (10.6km) with a wide variety of boats.
- Mies plage (12.3km) (beach) 200m after the service station on the edge of Versoix where folks like to hang out and have BBQs or swim.
- Coppet Castle (14km)
- Céligny beach (17.8km)
- Port of Crans (19.2km)
- Nyon (22km) - castle, port, cobblestone streets

At the time of writing, it will cost 9CHF to bring your bike back from here (or 4.50CHF if you have a half-price travel card). The train station is up at the top end of the town centre.

1b. Geneva to Rolle (+11km (34km in all - one way)

Click on the link or copy the relevant QR code (chapter 17) to discover the route

https://goo.gl/maps/D6TqdeFrkpfSNGy56

The cycle path comes onto the main road after Nyon but is still clearly marked with the yellow broken lines.

Interesting rest points:

- Gland - Plage de la Dullive (29.1km)
- Plage de Bursinel (31.7 km)
- Rolle (34km) with a beautiful port and castle and a very pleasant walk along the popular lakefront.

An alternative route back: with a slight climb past the Rolle train station, and left along the route de l'Etraz you will pass through the 'vineyard' villages of Bursins, Luins, (Formula One driver Lewis Hamilton used to have a house here which I could never find!) and back to the lake at Gland. If you do not mind some small hills you can return via Trélex, Duillier to Nyon, or come back via Vich and Trélex and lower Duillier.

1c. Geneva to Morges (+26km (49.2km in all - one way)

Click on the link or copy the relevant QR code (chapter 17) to discover the route

https://goo.gl/maps/8Bkw7GHqEwRSwUCT6

Cyclists share the road with other users for short periods of time (use brown cycle signs)

Interesting rest points:

Lake-front village of St Prex (44.4km)

Morges - Parc de l'indépendance, a must during 'Tulip season'!

Morges - castle and port (you can take a boat here across to France or back towards Geneva).

For those who wish to go further, check out Lausanne, the Swiss Riviera lakeside towns including Montreux and the vineyard terraces of Lavaux. For the serious cyclist, who wants to cycle right around the lake with others there is the *Cyclotour du Leman* in May. Food and drink are available at key points.

9

Green country route

- 2a. Versoix-Divonne (FR) (9.5km)
- 2b. Include the 'equestrian country' of Cheserex and Gingins (19km)
- 2c. Include the Zoo in Le Vaud (30km)

2a. Divonne(FR) lake (9.5 km -one way)

C lick on the link or copy the relevant QR code (chapter 17) to discover the route
https://goo.gl/maps/kc9mXnSA7onQEwcQ9

Starting point - Versoix- Port Choiseul car park (+10.6 km from the Pont du Mt Blanc)

This route has some small hills and is on cycle paths, minor roads and agricultural cement paths. Most of the route is off-road and uses sections of the Swiss National Cycle Route number 50.

Follow the cycle path right to the Mies roundabout and then take left for Mies and Tannay. Take left at the roundabout in Tannay up past the *Ferme Les Morennes* and the *Dechetterie*. Then left and under the motorway past Jumbo at Chavannes taking right at the end of the road. Arriving at the next T junction, follow signs left for Divonne and after passing the Douane (customs) turn right at the first small roundabout and you will arrive at the lake.

Cycling around the lake is 2.5km and very safe for children. If you look closely there are alternative wheel options! There are also several special play areas.

If you decide this is your final destination, there are some wonderful restaurants in the town of Divonne!

2b. Chéserex/Gingins (+8km (17.9km in all - one way)

Click on the link or copy the relevant QR code (chapter 17) to discover the route

https://goo.gl/maps/gP9SpwX3p6NYDQM18

Leave the Divonne lake area by the North East exit and take the D984c road towards the quaint village of Crassier. There is a cycle path parallel to the main road on the right-hand side. In Crassier at the roundabout follow signs towards Borex and immediately left before the Creperie, then right onto the *chemin de Marly* and continue for around 1km. Take left on the *route de Tranchepied* and then right after 500m on the clearly marked asphalted road. At the end, take left up the *Route de Grens* and you will arrive in Chéserex. Keep left at the fork onto the *route de la Florettaz*. Soon you will come out into a beautiful green area with a golf course over on the left. Any direction left or right will keep you on the flat and there are several picnic areas. (Straight on will take you uphill eventually into an area with houses and onto the route de la Dole).

There is also an indoor swimming pool in Chéserex, should that be of interest.

2c. Le Vaud Zoo (+ 21km (30.6km in all - one way)

Click on the link or copy the relevant QR code (chapter 17) to discover the route

https://goo.gl/maps/x1kEb2FCVygCycv37

This section uses minor roads and involves hills.

On leaving Chéserex, take the main road to Gingins and on the far edge of the village, take the left fork onto the route de Givrins. Be careful crossing the main road (an alternative is to stay straight on the *route de Trelex* and left at the roundabout before taking right) into *La Délaissée*. You pass through Givrins, Genolier, Bassins. Take right after the Tamoil service station below Bassins onto the *rue du Cardelay* and *Burtigny* and then *Vollottaz*. Then take left at the *route des Arenys* and right onto the *Route du Bois Laurent* and you will arrive at La Garenne. Details for the zoo can be found at https://en.lagarenne.ch/

(Needless to say, most of the return will be downhill at least to Divonne!)

10

Countryside Loop

3a. Chavannes Loop (40km)

C lick on the link or copy the relevant QR code (chapter 17) to discover the route
https://goo.gl/maps/FnZ1nqcv9Vt4rfgr7

This route starts at Mont-Blanc bridge in Geneva and uses minor roads and some off-road cycle paths in agricultural areas.

Follow our Route 1a until Versoix. 250m after the Lake Geneva Hotel in Versoix take left onto the *route de Sauverny* and straight over at the top roundabout towards Sauverny. At the forest, turn right into the *chemin de la Bécassière* which meanders behind the Mies Sport centre until it comes out on the *Route de Tannay*. Take left past the *déchetterie*, left at the end and then immediately right before the motorway tunnel.

At the end of the road take the left turn for Divonne and crossing over the motorway bridge turn left for Chavannes-des-Bois. When you arrive in the village keep right for Sauverny which winds parallel to the border past a speed camera.

Take right over the bridge and into France and then left at the church, (chemin de Villard Dame) past the tennis courts. At the end of this road (which is closed to traffic on Sundays) turn right and follow the main road up to Versonnex Mairie (village hall). Take left towards the centre of the village and then follow signs left at the roundabout towards Collex-Bossy. Turn right after the café in Collex, onto the route de Vireloup, keeping straight on at the roundabout on the main road. Take the quieter Chemin de Saint-Oyend behind the Bison Farm (you can see them from both sides). Come back out to the route de Colovrex. Take left at the traffic lights, to cross the motorway towards Grand Saconnex. At the end of this road, you will come back out to Route de Ferney and take left down past the Place des Nations and back down to the lakefront to bring you back to the Mont Blanc bridge.

3b. Chavannes - Divonne Loop (41.3km)

Click on the link or copy the relevant QR code (chapter 17) to discover the route

https://goo.gl/maps/udRET9uoqmLFVEmL8

Follow the route above until Chavannes, then straight to Divonne and left at the first roundabout. Go straight over at the gendarmerie and left onto the piste cyclable at Arbère to Grilly. Keep straight on until Versonnex and left towards Collex-Bossy as above.

3c. Chavannes - Vesancy Loop (47.4km)

Click on the link or copy the relevant QR code (chapter 17) to discover the route

https://goo.gl/maps/TLabCE54zssJqqy19

Follow above until Chavannes then straight to Divonne and take the Gex road to the beautiful village of Vesancy (also see route 5c). It's worth it to hike on foot up to the church above the village with stunning views over the lake. Then follow Gex, Cessy and Versonnex to pick up the above ride.

11

South Pays de Gex Loop

The Rhone River near Collonges

- 4a. St Jean de Gonville-Dardagny-Satigny loop (28km)
- 4b. Peron loop (30.7km)
- 4c. Collonges-Chancy loop (48km)

4a. St Jean de Gonville-Dardagny-Satigny loop (28km)

Click on the link or copy the relevant QR code (chapter 17) to discover the route
https://goo.gl/maps/5xjUQBjBfWExoSgL7

This route starts at the CERN tram terminus (18) and uses minor roads with some hills.

At the CERN border crossing, keep left and use the cycle path towards St Genis Pouilly, using the cycle paths cross around the right side of the roundabout. Be careful at both crossing points and make sure cars have come to a complete stop. (there is a building project on the way which will make this junction much easier by creating a tunnel). Follow the road into St Genis Pouilly and up the hill past the theatre. At Charly's pub, take left and immediately right which brings you out on the road to Sergy. Use the cycle path in Sergy village for as long as it lasts and follow the road up into the village. (While our route takes us straight on past the church, the village's bakery just 200m up from the church on the right is very popular and is open long hours!)

Follow the road on to Thoiry (the steeper uphill only lasts for 2min!). The little church in Thoiry (on your left just after the bakery is interesting). At the far end of Thoiry take right for St Jean de Gonville and Peron at the roundabout. After the slight uphill into Fenières, and on exiting the village, signal left at the fork, to keep on the lower level to St Jean de Gonville (see 4b* for the alternative at this point).

Taking left in St-Jean itself (after 1.5km) you will come down to the main road where you take right and then after 160m take left at a sign that says Z.A. Baritella.

This will take you down under the dual carriageway, across the border and up through a forest route, past beautiful vineyards and down into the village of Dardagny which boasts of a castle (now the Mairie!). You may want to take a break in the Tea-Room in the second half of the village!

Make sure your brakes are working well before you venture down the Route du Mandement as, if you don't use them, you will be going well over 50km/h!

(If you want to see the Rhone river at this point, take a right before the bridge and turn left just after the tunnel as there are some cool walks down there at the 'Confluent de l'Allondon' and places to sit beside the very turquoise Rhone river near a viaduct).

Follow the winding road up to Russin. You will not be going much more than 10km/h up the hill, switch to an easy gear, and relax and get used to going slower. In less than 4min you will arrive in the village at the top! It's more or less flat from here back to Satigny! On the edge of Russin, a cycle path appears and will bring you into Satigny. From here you can stay straight on to Meyrin by the cycle path and take left up to the CERN to finish the loop. Alternatively, take left in Satigny past the Mairie and follow signs to Choully, a very quaint wine village with a castle and several vineyard domains. Taking right in the village you will come out of the village by a steep hill past several vineyards. At the bottom of the hill take left and you will cycle down a traffic-free road at the bottom of which you will be back in France! Take right along the cycle path towards St Genis Pouilly and then right to bring you back to the CERN.

4b. Peron loop (30.7km)

Click on the link or copy the relevant QR code (chapter 17) to discover the route

https://goo.gl/maps/TZ4LbRRxF4hxAssu6

Follow the above directions until mention of 4b. Take right at the fork, up the slight hill towards upper St Jean de Gonville, past the bakery and right again at the end. Stay on this road avoiding any right turns and you will come up a slight hill into beautiful meadowland towards Péron. The road is narrow so be careful (I often cycle this without meeting any cars!) After several bends, the road will start to slope down and into Péron. Just as it does, the road to the right will take you up to an interesting little village of Feigères and you can circle back down a steep hill to St Jean de Gonville. Once in Péron, you can come back the same way, or choose to take the lower main road back in St Jean keeping the disused railway line on your left, past Val Thoiry and join the cycle path at Badian.

4c. Collonges-Chancy loop (48km)

Click on the link or copy the relevant QR code (chapter 17) to discover the route

https://goo.gl/maps/1yAkmEsPXoK4txRz9

Continue on to Farges and Collonges either on the lower main road or the smaller upper parallel road. From Collonges go downhill over the roundabout before the start of the main dual carriageway and follow the road down to Pougny to Chancy (CH) (alternatively you can join

Chancy directly from Farges). Having crossed back into Switzerland you can come back through Cartigny and/or Avully and pick up the road to Russin at that stage and join the end of Route 4a above to bring you back to the CERN.

12

North Pays de Gex Loop

Source de l'Allondon

- 5a. Source de l'Allondon loop (10km in all)
- 5b. Source de l'Allondon-Sauverny loop (24.5km in all)
- 5c. Allondon-Vesancy loop (38km in all)

5a. Source de l'Allondon loop (10km in all)

C lick on the link or copy the relevant QR code (chapter 17) to discover the route
https://goo.gl/maps/piuQum3znswXuTiRA

Starting point: St Genis Pouilly Intermarché (Add an extra 5.7km from CERN). This route is on minor roads with small hills.

Leaving Intermarché, take left towards the mountains and follow the road past the Jivahill Hotel resort, Crozet village and straight over a roundabout to the Source de l'Allondon (keeping the boulangerie to your right). The source is a beautiful wooded area with rivers, a potential waterfall (depending on the time of year) and a beautiful calm, shaded natural park area to relax in. Enter the park just after the bridge before the hill up to Naz-Dessous. Lock your bikes here near the bridge and go off and enjoy the park. When you come back to this same point, cycle up to the left into the village of Naz-Dessous and turn right to come back by Chevry and along to Intermarché.

5b. Source de l'Allondon-Sauverny loop (24.5km in all)

Click on the link or copy the relevant QR code (chapter 17) to discover the route
https://goo.gl/maps/EKYczhoDKFbjQgEBA

Follow 5a to visit the source de l'Allondon. In the village of Naz-Dessous take left and immediately right for Echenevex above the golf course. After passing through Echenevex, take left at the bottom of the hill towards Gex and straight over into the little road at Mury. After the small hamlet of Mury you will come out onto another main road (turning right). Then go straight over the Gex-Ferney road roundabout into Cessy and after the church take right towards Sauverny and keep straight on. (At the Chemin Levé crossroads, there is a small lake off to the left and a chance to relax with a short walk around the lake). Take right at the roundabout before Sauverny and come back to Versonnex and Maconnex before taking left and then right towards St Genis Pouilly. This will take you through the villages of Bretigny, Véraz and Pregnin before bringing you back up to Intermarché.

5c. Allondon-Vesancy loop (38km in all)

Click on the link or copy the relevant QR code (chapter 17) to discover the route

https://goo.gl/maps/wwyMv5pyS7c3bnoT7

For the more serious cyclist, follow the above route to the Allondon and Echenevex and then left to Gex. At the top of Gex, take left up towards the Mairie and then before arriving at the Mairie, follow the road to the right and over the junction towards the beautiful little village of Vesancy. It's worth parking your bikes in Vesancy village to hike up to the church above the village with stunning views over the lake. Cycle on to the upmarket town of Divonne and then right towards Ferney-Voltaire which will bring you through the quaint village of Grilly (with an interesting castle) and on to Versonnex where you will pick up the 5b route above to bring you back to St Genis Pouilly.

13

Vineyard Loop

- 6a. Meyrin-Russin loop (17.2km in all)
- 6b. Meyrin-Avully loop (26.3km in all)
- 6c. Meyrin-Chancy loop (40km in all)

6a. Meyrin-Russin loop (17.2km in all)

Click on the link or copy the relevant QR code (chapter 17) to discover the route
https://goo.gl/maps/4jmJfEA42nXUdWYs7

Starting point: Meyrin Village Tram stop (18). This route is mostly flat with some hills.

Cycle down the hill towards the CERN and cross over to the left just before the roundabout to stay on the cycle path towards Satigny. Take right at the route de Bourdigny roundabout and follow signs up to Bourdigny village taking your time to enjoy the vineyards on both sides. At the top end of Bourdigny, take left up the hill to Choully, a small wine village with several domaines. (You may want to walk up this hill). Keep straight on past the water tower and follow the road meandering down to Peissy. Turn left at the café des Amis towards Russin taking right at the roundabout at the bottom after passing the red house! (Route de Maison Rouge). The village of Russin offers a safe stopping point from which you come back along the main road (the cycle path appears again before Satigny) and back to Meyrin.

6b. Meyrin-Avully loop (25km in all)

Click on the link or copy the relevant QR code (chapter 17) to discover the route

https://goo.gl/maps/zTQSGEBtJvFLWCGk7

After Russin, take the hill down to Avully (check your brakes before moving!) and follow left for Cartigny and Aire la Ville before crossing the Rhone at the Pont de Peney. While each of these villages has cafés, you might like to stop at the Café de Peney before the short climb back to Satigny and return on the cycle path to Meyrin.

6c. Meyrin-Chancy loop (40km in all)

Click on the link or copy the relevant QR code (chapter 17) to discover the route

https://goo.gl/maps/Zozh3Vfonx3g23CDA

This more ambitious and hilly route includes the beautiful green areas of Malval and Dardagny (mentioned in route 4a). After Avully, it takes you right out to the border village of Chancy before swinging back to Cartigny and Aire la Ville.

14

South Lakeside to Yvoire

7. South Lakeside to Yvoire (FR) (28.7km one way)

C lick on the link or copy the relevant QR code (chapter 17) to discover the route
https://goo.gl/maps/6FzYoEn2WnxWQY3e7

Starting point: Pont du Mont-Blanc, Geneva. This route is almost entirely flat using both cycle paths and minor roads and passes through urban and country areas.

Follow the cycle path on the south side of Lac Léman, taking left in Vésenaz towards Hermance. On the edge of Collonge-Bellerive, there is a small beach at la Savonnière, behind the hospital. Crossing the border into France on the edge of Hermance (which has its own lake side *buvette*), the route soon brings you to the junction in Véreitre, from which you can take left down to the *Tougues* beach and port area (18.4km). The *plage de Messery* (23.4km) is another 'grass beach' area which overlooks the lake towards Nyon, as does Nernier port, 2km before arriving at the wonderful medieval village of Yvoire. With its numerous 'artisanal' shops and restaurants, Yvoire is very popular and demands at least a two-hour visit! Why not relax along the front before returning by, either the same road or by taking your bike on the CGN boat across to Nyon and cycling back the 20km from there to Mont Blanc or alternatively taking your bike on the train.

15

Salève Loop

8. Salève Loop (29 km in all)

(8.9km uphill. Elevation: 400m-1280m)

Click on the link or copy the relevant QR code (chapter 17) to discover

the route
https://goo.gl/maps/BVtB86QQNU9VVZ966

This route starts and ends at the Télépherique du Salève car park. (Add 7.5km from Mont Blanc bridge to starting point). The route uses minor roads after the initial 5km on normal roads.

Follow the road along to Etrembieres, leading onto the D2 and then up the *route du 8 mai* (D906A becomes the D15 and then the D41A).

I suggest taking the *route des 3 lacs* onto the *chemin des carrières* to come up to the Observatoire. The most interesting way to come down is to go straight on to *La Croisette* with its two small cafe restaurants (worth a stop!), before turning right onto the D45 steep hill back down towards the Télépherique car park. Take right at the bottom past the Bossey Golf Club, left on the *Chemin de Crevin* across the motorway and then right along to the Télépherique du Salève car park.

16

Col de la Faucille

It can be pretty snowy from December to February!

- 9a. Col de la Faucille (10.8km one way)
- 9b. Col de la Faucille-Les Rousses (28.4km in all - one way)
- 9c. Col de la Faucille-St Cergue loop (66km in all)

9a. Col de la Faucille (10.8km one way) Elevation: 600m to 1300m.

C lick on the link or copy the relevant QR code (chapter 17) to discover the route
https://goo.gl/maps/FZAwtFRHrGhpgYVx9

(Add 8.9km from Intermarché in St Genis). The starting point for this route is the café Cocottes Gessienes in upper Gex. (Car park (Perdtemps) is just past the café).

This route is entirely uphill and shares the D1005 with all other road users.

Follow the main road up to la Faucille passing the *Refuge du Florimont* restaurant (very popular and so better to have a reservation) with a fantastic panorama view from the car park. You will pass Napoleon's fountain, Belvedere des Pailly (with a breathtaking view of Mont Blanc), the Mainaz Hotel and finally make it to the top of la Faucille. Taking left, you will arrive at the Monts Jura ski station which also offers several different activities, including a zip line, 4 season luge, trotinnettes, mountain bikes (VTT) etc. There are also several cafés, a crêperie and views of the Jura. The return cycle back down (don't forget to look for Mont Blanc just before you meet the main road!) is not for the faint-hearted although some might say that you are basically sitting on a saddle and pulling the brakes!

(There is an alternative route up from Gex suited to mountain bikes via *le Creux de l'Envers, chemin de la noyelle, route des Seblines,* and back out at the *Belvedere des Pailly*).

9b. Col de la Faucille-Les Rousses (+18.5km (28.4km in all - one way)

Click on the link or copy the relevant QR code (chapter 17) to discover the route

https://goo.gl/maps/RN7rKCeYjkkSH385A

For those who wish to go further into the Jura, keep on towards Les Rousses, on what is a much flatter road (a further 18.5km and around 50min) and when you're ready come back the same way (57.6km return trip from start to finish). There are some great restaurants in Les Rousses which can get busy at peak times!

9c. Col de la Faucille-St Cergue loop (66km in all)

Click on the link or copy the relevant QR code (chapter 17) to discover the route

https://goo.gl/maps/JYwR5CfyuAzsawZt8

From Les Rousses, an alternative return route into Switzerland at La Cure will bring you through the quaint village of St-Cergue. The descent is windier than the Col de la Faucille but less steep as you head down towards Nyon. You can then return via Gingins and Divonne.

17

QR codes

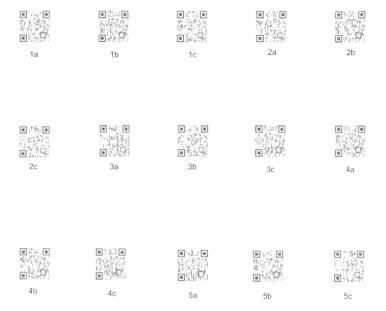

1a

1b

1c

2a

2b

2c

3a

3b

3c

4a

4b

4c

5a

5b

5c

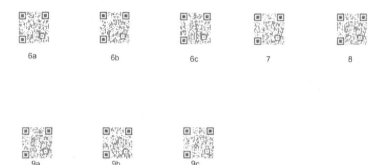

6a

6b

6c

7

8

9a

9b

9c

18

Restaurants en route

The following ideas do not represent an exhaustive list by any means but offer one or more options on each route. I have marked with an asterisk those that we have eaten in and can personally recommend.

Route 1 Céligny Buvette-(local speciality-Filet de perche)*

Route 2 Gingins-2 different *auberges*

Route 3 Divonne-l'Accord Parfait

Route 4 Thoiry-les Céphages/Dardagny-l'Auberge

Route 5. Crozet (near the télépherique)- Le Bois Joly Crozet*

Route 6 Russin café restaurant Vignoble-Doré

Route 7 Yvoire-too hard to choose!

Route 8. La Croisette-Les Marches de la Croisette*/Auberge des Montagnards*

Route 9. La Faucille-Crêperie *

19

Conclusion

T hanks for reading this short book. I hope you will be/have been able to try out more than one of my favourite routes and that the links were useful. I hope the weather is good and that you are able to enjoy your morning/day out. Whether you live in the area or you are visiting, I hope you keep fit and safe on the cycle paths and roads in the Greater Geneva area!

If you have found this little book helpful, I'd appreciate it greatly if you could give a favourable review on Amazon.

20

Resources

B ike Switzerland. (2021, March 1). *Book a Bike.* Retrieved February 13, 2022, from https://bikech.ch/rentals/

Geneva Cycling. (2022, February 1). *Road Bike Rental.* Retrieved May 13, 2022, from https://genevacycling.com/road-bike-rental/

Geneva Tourism. (2022, January 1). *Rent and Loan.* Https://Www.Geneveroule.Ch/En/. Retrieved February 13, 2022, from https://www.gen everoule.ch/en/rent-and-loan/

Google Maps short links or QR codes accessed according to Google Guidelines: https://about.google/brand-resource-center/products-a nd-services/geo-guidelines. Retrieved 13 May 2022 from https://map s.google.com

Office de Tourisme. (2022, February 1). *Pays de Gex, from the shores of Lake Geneva to the peak of the Jura mountains.* Pays de Gex & Sa Station

Monts Jura. Retrieved May 13, 2022, from https://www.paysdegex-montsjura.com/en/

Wells, M. (2016). *Cycling the River Rhone Cycle Route: From the Alps to the Mediterranean.* Cicerone Press Limited.

World climate guide. (2021, February 1). *Climate - Geneva (Switzerland).* Climates to Travel - World Climate Guide. Retrieved May 13, 2022, from https://www.climatestotravel.com/climate/switzerland/geneva

Printed in Great Britain
by Amazon